BEYOND
PRESSURE COOKER

Project Editor: Lisa M. Tooker

Translator: Christie Tam

Editor: Lynda Zuber Sassi

Design & Typography: Elizabeth M. Watson

Layout & Production: Patty Holden

Photography & Recipes: Teubner Foodfoto Jmbh

Printed in China

ISBN: 1-59637-023-8

CONTENTS

SEAFOOD

BEEF, LAMB, AND PORK

POULTRY AND GAME

RICE AND VEGETABLES

SOUPS AND STEWS

INTRODUCTION

Who would have thought that Aunt Ethel's pressure cooker would return to fashion? The new generation of pressure cookers is very different than Aunt Ethel's, but pressure cooking is becoming the rage once again. Gone are the days of the cooker jiggling on the stovetop, steam spitting and hissing, rattling like a vessel ready for lift off. While the vintage cooker may still be functional, it is probably better treasured as a family heirloom. Today's cookers range in size, brand, and cost, and they have feature advancements, including improved valve mechanisms, multiple safety systems, and enhanced adjustable cooking settings that make upgrading worthwhile.

As our lives become more hectic and there is less time available to prepare healthy, satisfying meals every night, pressure cookers are stepping up to the plate. Home cooks are turning to, or in some cases, returning to, pressure cooking as a solution to providing meals for their family. With the versatility of being able to prepare dishes such as Chicken Chili Con Carne (page 66), to Lamb Vindaloo (page 42), to Fillet of Sole on a Bed of Vegetables (page 24), it is no wonder that the pressure cooker is making a comeback.

BEHIND THE SCENES

Simply stated, a pressure cooker works by building up steam in a pot which creates pressure that cooks the food at a very high temperature; thus reducing cooking time. When the cooker's lid is locked into place and the cooking liquid begins to boil, the steam that is generated is literally trapped inside the pot with nowhere to go except through the food. The fibers and molecules in the food are broken down quickly, and as a result, cooking occurs in record time.

For example, when the cooker is operating at high pressure, 15psi (pounds per square inch), and the liquid boils at 250°F, rather than the standard boiling temperature of 212°F, the fibers in the food break down faster (in half to one-third of the time) than it would take to cook in a more conventional way. The same goes for low pressure, 8psi, or medium pressure, 10psi.

Other added benefits of pressure cooking are that fewer vitamins and nutrients are lost during the process because the steam condenses in the pot instead of escaping into the air, and food remains juicy, tender, and flavorful.

SIZING IT UP

Before taking the plunge and purchasing a new pressure cooker, consider its intended uses. Pressure cookers come in three standard sizes, four quart, six quart, and eight quart. These sizes reflect the total capacity that the cooker has inside. The actual useable capacity is two-thirds of the size since one-third needs to remain empty in order to accommodate the steam. As a rule of thumb, a four-quart cooker is a good size for small dishes, side dishes, or singles. A six-quart cooker is a good size for soups, small dishes, and small families and an eight-quart cooker is a good size for large families, canning, or cooking whole chickens and large roasts. If you're having trouble making up your mind about size, just remember, you can always make less in a larger cooker; making more in a smaller cooker is impossible.

Once you've selected the appropriate size cooker, you will choose between aluminum or stainless steel. Aluminum cookers are less expensive and weigh less than their stainless counterparts. Stainless steel cookers are more expensive and heavier than aluminum, but their durability and ability to hold heat longer makes them a smart choice. Stainless cookers are also less likely to burn food on the bottom.

SPEAKING THE LANGUAGE

Pressure cooking has a unique language of its own. Here are some common terms that you will find throughout this book.

COVER AND LOCK THE LID INTO PLACE: After adding the ingredients, you need to lock the lid into place. Refer to the manufacturer's directions to see how to perform this function properly with your cooker. Usually there are markers to line up and the lid clicks into place.

OVER HIGH HEAT: Place the cooker over a burner that is the same size as its bottom, not larger. Turn the burner to high. Bringing the cooker to high pressure will take between 30 seconds to 15–20 minutes, depending on the amount of ingredients in the cooker and the temperature of the cooking liquid.

BRING TO HIGH/MEDIUM/LOW PRESSURE: Refer to the manufacturer's directions to determine how high/medium/low pressure is indicated. New cookers will have a bar that indicates the pressure range and with the older, jiggle cookers; the regulator will begin to rock. The time it takes to bring the pressure up is not calculated in the recipe's cooking time.

LOWER AND ADJUST THE HEAT TO MAINTAIN EVEN PRESSURE: Once desired pressure is reached, lower the heat on the burner in order to maintain that level of pressure. If cooking times are long, you may need to make adjustments in the heat periodically to maintain even cooking pressure.

COOK UNDER PRESSURE FOR XX MINUTES: Once the desired level of pressure is reached, the actual cooking time begins. Refer to the recipe and/or to the manufacturer's directions to become familiar with cooking times.

RELEASE METHODS: There are three ways to release pressure once cooking has been completed—the quick release, the cold water release, and the natural release. These methods are described in detail later in this chapter.

CAREFULLY REMOVE THE LID: This final step is the most important for your safety. When removing the lid, a rush of steam will come out. Unlock the lid and turn it away from your face and body as you remove it from the cooker so the steam goes in the opposite direction.

COOKING TIMES

On average, it takes a pressure cooker half to one-third the time of more conventional cooking methods like baking, grilling, or braising. You will want to refer to the time charts in the manufacturer's instruction manual in addition to the recipes in this book. As you become familiar with your cooker, timing will become intuitive.

When cooking multiple ingredients at the same time, begin timing with the food that takes the longest to cook and add additional ingredients along the way. Or, cut the ingredients that take longer to cook into smaller pieces so they will cook at the same pace. Find a balance between size and time that works best for the recipe.

At the end of the day, there are five variables to consider when determining the cooking time for any pressure cooker recipe. 1. The size of the pot. 2. What the pot is made of, an aluminum pot is going to cook at a different rate of time than stainless steel. 3. The amount of liquid inside the pot. 4. The amount of ingredients, their shape, and quality; and 5. The type of heat source, is it gasor electric?

ADAPTING RECIPES

Once confident with the cooker, conventional recipes are easy to adapt. A rule of thumb to convert a standard recipe is to divide the cooking time by three. A recipe that would take 30 minutes will take roughly 10 minutes in the cooker. The first time you try it, err on the side of a shorter cooking time. If more time is needed bring the cooker back to pressure and cook for a few more minutes.

HIGH ALTITUDE

Using a pressure cooker in high altitudes is easy; it just requires a few math skills. The formula that calculates for lower external pressure at elevations above 2000 feet is: for every 1000 feet above 2000 feet elevation, increase cooking time by five percent.

RELEASE METHODS

QUICK RELEASE OR TOUCH METHOD: This feature found in new cookers allows you to reduce pressure without losing heat with the touch of a button. It is the best method for checking for doneness or when adding ingredients. If more cooking time is needed, simply lock the lid back into place and build up pressure. Since the cooker hasn't cooled off, it will quickly return to pressure and continue cooking. This method is energy efficient, economical, and time saving. An additional benefit of the quick release method is that it can all be done on the stovetop; there is no need to carry the cooker to the sink.

COLD WATER RELEASE METHOD: This method is the quickest way to stop the cooking process. Move the cooker to the sink and turn it at a 45 degree angle, away from your body, then run cold water over the top and down the side. Avoid running water over the valve. Cooking stops almost immediately. The cold water release is the method of choice for vegetables and risotto, where cooking times are short and the possibility of overcooking easy.

NATURAL RELEASE METHOD: The natural release method requires removing the cooker from the heat and letting the pressure drop on its own. Food will continue to cook inside as the pressure drops. Natural pressure is used in meat recipes as it keeps meat tender and juicy. Natural release is also used with beans and grains. A good rule of thumb is for every 4 minutes of time cooking under pressure, it will take 10 minutes for the steam to release naturally. Natural release time is not calculated in the recipes.

TROUBLESHOOTING

If for some reason, the cooker's lid does not come off easily, DO NOT force it. It is likely that there is still pressure inside. Put it back on the heat and bring it up to a small amount of pressure, then use the quick release method to let off the residual pressure, and pop it open. If you have a jiggle top, put it back on the stove and bring up to a small amount of pressure. Use the cold water release method to drop the pressure and remove the lid.

CARE AND CLEANING

The final component to pressure cooking is the care and cleaning of the cooker. While the pressure cooker requires more care than a regular stock pot, proper care is not complicated and will add to your cooker's longevity.

GASKET AND LID: Immediately after use, remove the gasket and wash the lid by hand. In order to preserve the life span of the gasket, allow it to dry thoroughly before returning it to the lid. If you notice that the cooker has become difficult to turn when closing, it is likely that the gasket is drying out. Try rubbing it with cooking oil to moisturize and revitalize. Give special attention to the rim of the lid and be sure that it is scrubbed free of residual food.

VALVE AND VENTS: Check the valve and vent areas and scrub them free of remaining food. From time to time, you may want to take the valve and vents apart. Refer to the manufacturer's directions when doing so and make sure that everything is screwed in tightly when replaced.

THE BOTTOM: If the bottom of your cooker has remnants of the last meal stuck to it, or if it has become lackluster and scorched over time, try soaking it in dish soap and hot water overnight. Scrub the bottom with a non-abrasive pad or brush. If the stains are stubborn, boil the water and scrape the bottom like you're de-glazing a pan. White stains are a sign of calcium deposits from hard water, or starch deposits from rice or beans. These deposits are best removed with a few drops of vinegar or lemon juice mixed with water and scrubbed with a non-abrasive pad or brush.

STORAGE: Once the cooker and gasket are dry, either set the lid upside down on top of the cooker—leaving some room for ventilation, or if you have extra storage space, set the lid and cooker side-by-side. Never lock the lid in place or the aromas and flavors of your last meal will be married to your next!

SEAFOOD

COOKING SEAFOOD in a pressure cooker results in moist and tender fish. Whether served in a soup or a stew, with a side of rice or on top of vegetables, seafood dishes made in a pressure cooker are quick, easy, and nutritious.

Cooking times will vary depending on what type of seafood you are preparing so refer to the manufacturer's instructions and the time in the recipes in this chapter. If you are cooking fish on its own, grease the bottom of the steamer basket or trivet so it doesn't stick. Making fish in a pressure cooker is the perfect one pot meal.

Salmon and Vegetable Soup

1 lb red new potatoes, cubed
½ cup carrots, chopped
½ cup leeks, sliced
5 cups fish stock
2 bay leaves
½ cup petite peas (frozen)
½ lb salmon fillet, skin removed
2 tbs chopped chervil
½ cup heavy cream
Zest from ½ lemon
Chervil for garnish
Kosher salt
Freshly ground black pepper

IN A PRESSURE COOKER, combine potatoes, carrots, leeks, stock, and bay leaves. Season with salt and pepper, simmer for 5 minutes, and then add the peas and salmon.

LOCK THE COOKER'S LID into place and bring to high pressure, 15psi, according to manufacturer's directions. Cook for 8–10 minutes, then lower the heat, and adjust as necessary to maintain even cooking pressure. Allow the pressure to drop naturally or with the quick release feature and carefully remove the lid.

USING A SLOTTED SPOON, remove the salmon and break it into large, bite-sized chunks then set aside. Add chervil, cream, and lemon to the cooker and simmer 3–4 minutes, stirring. Return the salmon to the cooker and season with salt and pepper.

TO SERVE: Divide soup into bowls and garnish with additional chervil.

SERVES 4

Spicy Fish Soup

2 tbs sesame oil
3 stalks lemon grass
½ tsp red pepper flakes
2 garlic cloves, minced
1 tbs freshly grated ginger root
½ cup carrots, cut into strips
½ cup red bell peppers, cut
    into strips
2 cups chicken stock
12 oz tomato juice
2 tomatoes, cut into strips
½ tsp curry
½ tsp cumin
Dash of soy sauce
2 sole fillets (about 6 oz), cut
    into 2 inch cubes
2 red snapper fillets (about 6 oz),
    cut into 2 inch cubes
1 tbs chopped cilantro

HEAT THE OIL in the pressure cooker and sauté the lemon grass, red pepper flakes, garlic, ginger, carrot, and bell pepper. Add the stock, tomato juice, and tomatoes.

LOCK THE COOKER'S LID into place and heat according to manufacturer's instructions to high pressure, 15psi, and cook for 3–4 minutes. Lower the heat and adjust as necessary to maintain even cooking pressure. Allow the pressure to drop naturally or with the quick release feature and carefully remove the lid.

ADD THE CURRY, cumin, soy sauce, and fish. Lock the lid once again and bring up to high pressure for 5 minutes. Allow the pressure to drop using the quick release method, remove the lid, and serve garnished with cilantro.

SERVES 4

TIP

► If the soup is too spicy, add a little coconut milk to mellow it out.

Cabbage Soup
with Shrimp

3 tbs vegetable oil, separated
2 tbs minced onions
1 garlic clove, minced
½ lb white cabbage, cut into strips
1 cup red and green bell peppers,
    cut into strips
½ tsp Hungarian sweet paprika
4 cups vegetable stock
8 raw medium-sized shrimp, peeled
1 tbs chopped parsley
Kosher salt
Freshly ground black pepper

IN A PRESSURE COOKER, heat 2 tablespoons of oil and sauté the onions and garlic until translucent. Add the cabbage, bell peppers, paprika, and stock, and season with salt and pepper.

COVER AND LOCK the cooker's lid into place and bring to low pressure, 8psi, according to manufacturer's instructions, and cook for 7 minutes. Lower the heat and adjust as necessary to maintain even cooking pressure. Allow the pressure to drop using the quick release feature and carefully remove the lid.

IN THE MEANTIME, heat the remaining oil in a separate pan and sauté the shrimp until pink, about 3–4 minutes.

TO SERVE: Place 2 shrimp in each bowl and pour the soup over the top. Garnish with parsley.

SERVES 4

Shrimp and Carrot Soup

2 tbs vegetable oil
½ cup white onion, cut into strips
1 cup carrots, cut into strips
1 leek, white parts only, cut
    into rings
½ cup red bell peppers, diced
1 cup red new potatoes, diced
4 cups vegetable stock
⅓ lb cooked shrimp, peeled
1 tbs chopped dill
Kosher salt
Freshly ground black pepper

IN A PRESSURE COOKER, heat the oil and sauté the onions until translucent, then add the carrots, leeks, bell peppers, potatoes, and stock. Lock the cooker's lid into place and build up to high pressure, 15psi, according to manufacturer's directions and cook for 4–5 minutes. Lower the heat and adjust as necessary to maintain even cooking pressure. Using the quick release feature, allow the pressure to drop and carefully remove the lid.

STIR IN THE SHRIMP and season to taste with salt and pepper. Simmer for 3–5 minutes until the shrimp is warm.

TO SERVE the Shrimp and Carrot Soup, pour it into bowls and garnish with dill.

SERVES 4

New England Clam Chowder

4 cans chopped clams (about
    6½ oz each)
2½ cups vegetable stock
3½ oz bacon
½ cup celery, chopped
½ cup shallots, minced
1 lb red new potatoes, peeled
    and diced
8 oz corn (canned or frozen)
1½ cups milk
1½ cups half and half
1 tbs chopped thyme
Kosher salt
Freshly ground black pepper

DRAIN THE CLAMS, reserving the liquid. Add the liquid to the stock and set the clams aside.

IN THE PRESSURE COOKER, fry the bacon until crispy, then remove, drain on a paper towel, and crumble into pieces. Add the celery and shallots to the pot and sauté in the bacon grease 3–5 minutes, add the potatoes, thyme, and stock with clam liquid. Season with salt and pepper and bring to a boil.

LOCK THE COOKER'S LID into place and bring up to high pressure, 15psi, according to manufacturer's directions and cook for 5 minutes. Lower the heat and adjust as necessary to maintain even cooking pressure. Allow the pressure to drop naturally or with the quick release feature and carefully remove the lid.

ADD THE CORN, milk, half and half, and reserved clams. Simmer, but do not boil, until everything is heated through, about 5–10 minutes, and season to taste with salt and pepper.

SERVE NEW ENGLAND CLAM CHOWDER in bowls garnished with thyme and sourdough bread on the side.

SERVES 4

Stewed Calamari

2½ lb calamari, cleaned
½ cup olive oil
½ cup white onions, diced
3 garlic cloves, minced
28 oz diced tomatoes
½ cup white wine
⅓ cup fish stock
1 tbs chopped parsley
1 tbs chopped basil
Kosher salt
Freshly ground black pepper

RINSE THE CALAMARI and pat dry. Heat the olive oil in the bottom of the pressure cooker and sauté the onions and garlic 3–5 minutes. Add the tomatoes, wine, and stock.

LOCK THE COOKER'S LID in place, bring up to high pressure, 15psi, according to manufacturer's directions, and cook for 7–10 minutes. Lower the heat and adjust as necessary to maintain even cooking pressure. Using the cold release method, allow the pressure to drop and carefully remove the lid.

STIR IN THE PARSLEY and basil and season with salt and pepper.

SERVE CALAMARI in bowls garnished with additional basil and parsley.

SERVES 4

Fillet of Sole on a Bed of Vegetables

½ cup carrots, grated
½ cup zucchini, grated
½ cup broccoli florets
½ cup mushrooms, sliced
1 tsp nutmeg
½ lb fillet of sole
½ cup white wine
½ cup lemon juice
Parsley for garnish
Kosher salt
Freshly ground black pepper

PLACE THE COOKER'S TRIVET or a steamer basket in the bottom of the pressure cooker. In a bowl, combine the carrots, zucchini, broccoli, and mushrooms, seasoning with nutmeg, salt, and pepper then add to the pressure cooker.

RINSE THE SOLE and pat dry, then season with salt and pepper. Place on top of the vegetables. Finally, pour the wine and lemon juice over the top.

LOCK THE COOKER'S LID in place, bring up to high pressure, 15psi, according to manufacturer's directions, and cook for 3–5 minutes. Lower the heat and adjust as necessary to maintain even cooking pressure. Using the cold water release method, allow the pressure to drop and carefully remove the lid.

REMOVE THE SOLE and vegetables from the cooker and arrange on a platter. Drizzle some of the juices over the top and garnish with parsley.

SERVE WITH A GREEN SALAD and roasted potatoes on the side.

SERVES 2

BEEF, LAMB, AND PORK

COOKING MEAT IN A PRESSURE COOKER is the perfect way for busy cooks to prepare savory, flavorful, and healthy meals in record time. Recipes in this section use flavored cooking liquids such as meat stock and feature a variety of herbs, spices, and other seasonings that contribute to infusing flavor. Cooking times will vary based on the type of meat, the quality, and size. Use the times in these recipes as guidelines, and as you get to know your pressure cooker, modify and make adjustments. When in doubt, use a meat thermometer and always err on the side of undercooking.

Hearty Beef Stew

2 lb beef, cubed for stew
½ cup olive oil
½ cup onions, chopped
2 garlic cloves, minced
½ cup carrots, sliced
½ cup eggplant, cubed
½ cup yellow zucchini, sliced
½ lb red new potatoes, sliced
8 oz diced tomatoes
1 tsp red pepper flakes
1 tbs tomato paste
½ cup white wine
1 cup beef stock
1 tbs chopped parsley
Kosher salt
Freshly ground black pepper

IN A BOWL, season the beef with salt and pepper. Heat the oil in the pressure cooker and brown the beef on all sides. Remove the beef and set aside, then sauté the onions and garlic 3–5 minutes. Return the beef to the cooker and add carrots, eggplant, zucchini, potatoes, tomatoes, red pepper flakes, tomato paste, wine, and stock.

LOCK THE COOKER'S LID in place and bring up to high pressure, 15psi, according to manufacturer's directions. Lower the heat and adjust as necessary to maintain even cooking pressure. When pressure is reached, lower the heat and cook for 15–20 minutes. Allow the pressure to drop naturally and carefully remove the lid.

SERVE THE STEW in bowls garnished with parsley and accompanied by a medium-bodied red wine.

Beer Braised Beef

2½ lb stewing beef, cubed
2 tbs canola oil, separated
1 large onion, sliced
2 garlic cloves, minced
2 medium carrots, cut
   into sticks
½ cup brown button
   mushrooms, sliced
½ tsp ground allspice
1 large bay leaf
1 small cinnamon stick
12 oz dark Bavarian beer
2 tbs chopped parsley
Kosher salt
Freshly ground black pepper

IN A PRESSURE COOKER, brown the beef in half the oil for 5 minutes. Remove with a slotted spoon and set aside.

ADD THE REMAINING oil and sauté the onion and garlic for 3–5 minutes. Stir in the carrots and mushrooms; add the allspice, bay leaf, and cinnamon stick. Return the beef to the cooker, stir in the beer, and season with salt and pepper.

LOCK THE COOKER'S LID into place and bring up to high pressure, 15psi, according to manufacturer's directions. When pressure is reached, lower the heat and adjust as necessary to maintain even cooking pressure, and cook for 15–20 minutes. Allow the pressure to drop naturally and carefully remove the lid.

DISCARD THE BAY LEAF and cinnamon stick. Serve the stew in bowls and sprinkle with parsley.

SERVES 4

Hungarian Goulash

2 lb stewing beef, cut into
  1 inch cubes
1 tbs Hungarian sweet paprika
2 tbs olive oil
1 cup onions, chopped
1 cup beef stock, separated
½ cup sauerkraut (prepared)
1 tsp caraway seeds
1 tbs tomato paste
½ cup sour cream
1 tbs chopped parsley
Kosher salt
Freshly ground black pepper

RINSE THE BEEF and pat dry; season with paprika, salt, and pepper. In a pressure cooker, heat the olive oil and brown the meat on all sides. Remove and set aside, then sauté the onions 3–5 minutes. Return the meat to the pressure cooker and add half of the stock.

LOCK THE COOKER'S LID in place and bring up to high pressure, 15psi, according to manufacturer's directions. When pressure is reached, lower the heat and cook for 5–7 minutes, adjusting the heat as necessary to maintain even cooking pressure. Allow the pressure to drop naturally and carefully remove the lid.

IN A BOWL, combine the sauerkraut and caraway seeds then stir into the cooker. Add the remaining stock, tomato paste, and season to taste with salt and pepper. Lock the lid in place and bring up to high pressure and cook for 10 more minutes. Allow the pressure to drop naturally.

SERVE THE GOULASH in bowls garnished with a dollop of sour cream and parsley.

SERVES 4

Tri-Color Rice and Beef

⅔ lb stewing beef, cut into
    ½ inch cubes
2 tbs vegetable oil
2 tbs green onions, sliced
    into rings
1 garlic clove, minced
1 tsp red pepper flakes
½ cup bell peppers (red, yellow,
    and or green), diced
8 oz diced tomatoes
½ cup long-grain rice
1 tsp Hungarian sweet paprika
1 tbs tomato paste
1 cup beef stock
1 tbs chopped parsley
Kosher salt
Freshly ground black pepper

RINSE THE BEEF and pat dry; season with salt and pepper. Heat oil in the bottom of a pressure cooker and brown the beef on all sides. Remove the beef and set aside. Add the onions and garlic and sauté for 3–5 minutes, then add the red pepper flakes, bell peppers, tomatoes, rice, paprika, tomato paste, stock, beef, and season with salt and pepper.

LOCK THE COOKER'S LID in place and bring up to low pressure, 8psi, according to manufacturer's directions. When pressure is reached, lower the heat and adjust as necessary to maintain even cooking pressure, and cook for 5–7 minutes. Allow the pressure to drop naturally and carefully remove the lid.

SERVE IN BOWLS with parsley sprinkled on top.

SERVES 2

Stuffed Beef Roast

2½ lb rolled beef roast
½ cup carrots, sliced
½ cup leeks, white parts only, sliced
½ cup sliced celeriac (celery root)
3 tbs vegetable oil
½ cup onions, chopped
¼ cup celery, chopped
½ cup tomatoes, seeded and diced
1 bay leaf
2½ cups beef stock
Rosemary for garnish
Kosher salt
Freshly ground black pepper

USING A SHARP KNIFE, cut open the roast and fold it out flat; season with salt and pepper. Briefly blanch the carrots, leeks, and celeriac in boiling, salted water, then plunge into cold water and drain well. Place vegetables on top of the beef, roll up, and tie with kitchen string.

HEAT THE OIL in the pressure cooker, brown the roast on all sides, then remove and set aside. Add the onions and celery and sauté for 3–5 minutes. Add the roast, tomatoes, bay leaf, and stock.

LOCK THE COOKER'S LID in place and bring up to high pressure, 15psi, according to manufacturer's directions. When pressure is reached, lower the heat and cook for 35–40 minutes. Adjust the heat as necessary to maintain even cooking pressure. Allow the pressure to drop naturally and carefully remove the lid.

REMOVE THE ROAST and let it stand for 10 minutes. Pour the juices from the cooker through a strainer and into a sauce pan. Reduce slightly on the stovetop seasoning with salt and pepper.

TO SERVE: Slice the roast and drizzle the juices over the top. Garnish with rosemary and accompany with a side of roasted potatoes.

SERVES 4

Lamb Stew

1 lb lamb stew meat, cut into
    1 inch cubes

2 tbs vegetable oil

½ cup onions, chopped

1 garlic clove, minced

1 bay leaf

1 tsp chopped thyme leaves

4 cups beef or lamb stock

½ cup parsnips, peeled and cubed

½ cup rutabagas, peeled and cubed

½ cup carrots, peeled and cubed

1 tbs chopped thyme

Kosher salt

Freshly ground black pepper

RINSE THE LAMB, pat dry, and season with salt and pepper. Heat the oil in the bottom of a pressure cooker and brown the lamb on all sides. Remove the lamb and set aside, then sauté the onions and garlic 3–5 minutes. Return the lamb back to the pressure cooker and add the bay leaf, thyme, and stock.

LOCK THE COOKER'S LID into place and bring up to high pressure, 15psi, according to manufacturer's directions. When pressure is reached, lower the heat and cook for 10 minutes. Adjust the heat as necessary to maintain even cooking pressure. Allow the pressure to drop naturally and carefully remove the lid.

ADD THE PARSNIPS, rutabagas, and carrots, and season with salt and pepper. Lock the lid in place once again, bring back to high pressure, and cook for 5 more minutes. Allow the pressure to drop naturally and remove the lid.

TO SERVE: Divide the stew into bowls and garnish with thyme.

SERVES 4

Moroccan Lentils and Lamb

1 lb lamb stew meat, cubed
3 tbs olive oil
⅔ cup onions, chopped
2 garlic cloves, minced
½ tsp grated ginger
1 tsp cinnamon
½ tsp turmeric
2 cups lamb or beef stock
½ cup garbanzo beans
⅓ cup brown lentils
15 oz diced tomatoes
½ cup fresh spinach, cleaned
Mint leaves
Kosher salt
Freshly ground black pepper

RINSE THE LAMB, pat dry, and season with salt and pepper. Heat the oil in a pressure cooker, brown the lamb on all sides, then remove, and set aside. Add the onions and garlic and sauté for 3–5 minutes, then add the reserved lamb, ginger, cinnamon, and turmeric. Season with salt and pepper, stirring, and sauté for 3–5 more minutes.

ADD THE STOCK and lock the cooker's lid in place and bring up to high pressure, 15psi, according to manufacturer's directions. When pressure is reached, lower the heat and cook for 15 minutes. Adjust the heat as necessary to maintain even cooking pressure. Allow the pressure to drop naturally and carefully remove the lid.

ADD THE GARBANZO BEANS, lentils, and tomatoes. Lock the lid in place once again, bring up to high pressure, and cook for 5 more minutes. Allow the pressure to drop naturally and remove the lid.

STIR IN THE SPINACH until wilted, then serve in bowls and garnish with mint leaves.

SERVES 4

Lamb Vindaloo

Vindaloo paste

1 tbs coriander seeds

1 tsp cumin

4 whole cloves

1 cinnamon stick

1½ tsp black peppercorns

1 tbs fenugreek seeds

½ tsp black mustard seeds

1 tsp fennel seeds

½ tsp palm sugar

½ cup white vinegar

Lamb

2½ lb lamb stewing meat, cut
    into 1–1½ inch cubes

3 tbs ghee (or clarified butter)

½ cup onions, chopped

1 tbs freshly grated ginger root

5 garlic cloves, minced

5 tbs red chili peppers, cut in
    half and seeds removed

1 bay leaf

8 oz diced tomatoes

1 cup beef stock

Kosher salt

TOAST ALL OF THE SPICES in an ungreased pan for 4–5 minutes, until aromatic. Remove and let cool slightly. In a mortar, grind the spices and transfer to a bowl and combine with the vinegar to form a paste.

RINSE THE LAMB and pat dry. In a bowl, combine the lamb with the vindaloo paste, cover, and marinate for 4–5 hours.

IN A PRESSURE COOKER, heat the ghee (or clarified butter), and brown the lamb on all sides. Remove the lamb from the pan and set aside. Add the onions, ginger, garlic, and chili peppers and sauté for 3–4 minutes. Add the reserved lamb, bay leaf, tomatoes, and stock.

LOCK THE COOKER'S LID in place and bring up to high pressure, 15psi, according to manufacturer's directions. When pressure is reached, lower the heat and cook for 15 minutes. Adjust the heat as necessary to maintain even cooking pressure. Allow the pressure to drop naturally and carefully remove the lid.

SERVE THE LAMB over rice and toast your guests with a cold Indian beer.

SERVES 4

Pork and Vegetable Stew

2½ lb pork loin, cut into
    1 inch cubes
2 tbs olive oil
2 lb head of white cabbage,
    cut into strips
½ cup onions, cut into strips
3 garlic cloves, minced
½ cup carrots, chopped
1½ lb red new potatoes, peeled
    and halved
3 tbs chopped parsley
½ tsp caraway seeds
1½ cups vegetable stock
Parsley for garnish
Kosher salt
Freshly ground black pepper

RINSE THE PORK and pat dry; season with salt and pepper. Heat the olive oil in a pan and brown the pork on all sides.

ARRANGE A LAYER of cabbage in the bottom of a pressure cooker. Top it with the pork, followed by onions, garlic, carrots, and potatoes. Season with salt and pepper, then add parsley, and caraway seeds.

POUR THE STOCK over the top, lock the cooker's lid in place, and bring up to high pressure, 15psi, according to manufacturer's directions. Once pressure is reached, lower the heat and cook for 10–12 minutes. Adjust the heat as necessary to maintain even cooking pressure. Allow the pressure to drop naturally and carefully remove the lid.

REMOVE THE VEGETABLES and pork from the cooker and serve in bowls garnished with additional parsley.

SERVES 4

Apples, Pork, and Root Vegetables

⅔ lb boneless pork loin, cut
    into 1 inch cubes
1 tbs vegetable oil
½ cup onions, chopped
½ cup white wine
1 cup beef stock
½ cup rutabagas, peeled
    and diced
½ cup turnips, peeled
    and diced
½ cup carrots, diced
⅓ cup parsley root, peeled
    and diced
½ cup leeks, white parts
    only, sliced
½ tsp mild curry
1 tbs chopped thyme leaves
1 tbs chopped parsley
Juice from 1 lemon
½ cup Granny Smith apples,
    peeled and diced
Thyme for garnish
Kosher salt
Freshly ground black pepper

RINSE THE PORK and pat dry; season with salt and pepper. Heat the oil in the bottom of a pressure cooker and brown the pork on all sides. Remove the pork and set aside, then add the onions, and sauté 3–5 minutes. Return the pork to the cooker, and add the wine, stock, root vegetables, curry, thyme, parsley, and lemon juice and season with salt and pepper. Stir the ingredients together.

LOCK THE COOKER'S LID in place and bring up to high pressure, 15psi, according to manufacturer's directions. Once pressure is reached, lower the heat and cook for 10–15 minutes. Adjust the heat as necessary to maintain even cooking pressure. Allow the pressure to drop naturally and carefully remove the lid.

REMOVE THE LID and add the apples. Simmer for 5 minutes until apples become tender.

TO SERVE: Remove the pork and vegetables from the cooker and arrange in bowls. Drizzle juices over the top and garnish with thyme.

SERVES 4

Pork with Vegetables and Herb Rice

1⅓ lb pork round, sliced
3 tbs olive oil
1 garlic clove, minced
2 tbs chopped onions
⅓ cup bell peppers, diced
½ cup baby yellow zucchini, sliced
1 tsp red pepper flakes
2 tsp chopped black olives, pitted
1 tsp Hungarian sweet paprika
1 cup beef stock
Fresh herbs for garnish
Kosher salt
Freshly ground black pepper

Herb rice
1 tbs olive oil
2 tbs chopped white onions
1 garlic clove, minced
1 cup long-grain rice
1½ cups vegetable stock
2 tbs chopped parsley
2 tbs chopped chives
1 tbs chopped tarragon
1 tbs chopped basil

RINSE THE PORK and pat dry then season with salt and pepper. Heat the olive oil in the pressure cooker and brown the pork, piece-by-piece, setting it aside once browned. Add garlic and onions to the cooker and sauté 3–5 minutes. Add the bell peppers, zucchini, red pepper flakes, and olives. Return the reserved pork and season with paprika, salt, and pepper.

ADD THE STOCK, lock the cooker's lid in place, and bring up to high pressure, 15psi, according to manufacturer's directions. When pressure is reached, lower the heat and cook for 5 minutes. Allow the pressure to drop naturally and carefully remove the lid. Transfer the ingredients from the cooker to a platter and cover with aluminum foil to keep warm.

RINSE THE PRESSURE COOKER then make the rice. Heat the oil in the bottom of the cooker and sauté the onions and garlic 2–3 minutes. Add the rice and stock. Lock the cooker's lid in place and bring up to high pressure, and cook for 5 more minutes. Allow the pressure to drop naturally and remove the lid. Stir in herbs and season to taste with salt and pepper.

TO SERVE: Scoop the rice into bowls and top with pork and vegetables. Garnish with additional herbs.

SERVES 4

Pork Pot Roast

1⅓ lb pork shoulder, cut
    into 1 inch cubes
Juice from ½ lemon
2 tbs sunflower oil
½ cup onions, chopped
3 garlic cloves, minced
15 oz diced tomatoes
1 tbs tomato paste
1 tbs turmeric
½ tsp coriander
1 cup beef stock
1 tbs chopped parsley
Kosher salt
Freshly ground black pepper

RINSE THE PORK and pat dry; squeeze lemon juice over the top, season with salt and pepper, and set aside to marinate for 1 hour.

HEAT THE OIL in the pressure cooker, brown the pork on all sides, then remove, and set aside. Add the onions and garlic and sauté for 3–5 minutes, stir in the pork, tomatoes, tomato paste, turmeric, coriander, and stock.

LOCK THE COOKER'S LID in place and bring up to high pressure, 15psi, according to manufacturer's directions. When pressure is reached, lower the heat and cook for 10–15 minutes. Adjust the heat as necessary to maintain even cooking pressure. Allow the pressure to drop naturally and carefully remove the lid.

SERVE THE POT ROAST in shallow bowls garnished with parsley.

SERVES 2

Pork Roulades in Spicy Tomato Sauce

8 pork cutlets (about ½ lb each)
2–3 tbs Dijon mustard
8 thin slices smoked bacon
2–3 gherkins, sliced
½ cup white onions, cut
    into rings
2 tablespoons olive oil
1 garlic clove, minced
8 oz diced tomatoes
⅔ cup beef stock
Several basil leaves
Kosher salt
Freshly ground black pepper

8 toothpicks

RINSE THE PORK and pat dry. Place the pork between sheets of plastic wrap and hammer flat with a meat tenderizer. Place side-by-side on a work surface, season with salt and pepper, and spread a thin layer of mustard on each. Top each piece of pork with 1 slice of bacon, several gherkin slices, and onion rings. Roll up and secure with toothpicks.

HEAT THE OIL in a pressure cooker and brown the pork on all sides, then remove, and set aside. Add the garlic and sauté 3–5 minutes. Add the tomatoes, stock, and reserved pork, and season with salt and pepper.

LOCK THE COOKER'S LID into place and bring up to high pressure, 15psi, according to manufacturer's directions. When pressure is reached, lower the heat and cook for 10–15 minutes. Adjust the heat as necessary to maintain even cooking pressure. Allow the pressure to drop naturally and carefully remove the lid.

TO SERVE: Arrange the pork roulades on a platter and drizzle with the tomato sauce from the cooker. Garnish with basil leaves.

SERVES 4

POULTRY AND GAME

PREPARING POULTRY AND GAME in the pressure cooker lets you make your favorite comfort food, like Chicken Soup (page 58) in a fraction of the time it would traditionally take.

Cook most chicken and game dishes at high pressure, 15psi, and use the quick or cold release methods. The amount of cooking time will vary based on whether your bird is boneless, the size of the pieces, the leanness, and the quality. It is not always necessary to brown poultry and game before cooking, so if you're watching your waistline, forgo this step and your meal will still be tasty. Use a good chicken stock as a cooking liquid to add flavor. Since poultry and game has the tendency to dry out if overcooked, pay close attention to cooking times and be careful not to over cook.

Chicken, Rice, and Vegetables

1 lb boneless chicken breast
¼ cup vegetable oil, separated
½ cup onions, chopped
1 garlic clove, minced
15 oz diced tomatoes
1 tsp red pepper flakes
1½ cup chicken stock, separated
½ cup celery, chopped
½ cup eggplant, cubed
⅓ cup zucchini, cubed
1 cup long-grain rice
1 tbs chopped parsley
Kosher salt
Freshly ground black pepper

RINSE THE CHICKEN and pat dry. Using a sharp knife, cut the chicken into 1 inch cubes and season with salt and pepper. Heat 2 tablespoons of oil in the pressure cooker and brown the chicken on all sides. Remove the chicken and set aside. Add the onions and garlic and sauté for 3–5 minutes. Add the tomatoes, red pepper flakes, ½ cup of stock, and the reserved chicken; season with salt and pepper.

LOCK THE COOKER'S LID in place and bring up to high pressure, 15psi, according to manufacturer's directions. When pressure is reached, lower the heat and cook for 5 minutes. Adjust the heat as necessary to maintain even cooking pressure. Allow the pressure to drop using the quick release method and carefully remove the lid.

IN A PAN, heat the remaining oil and sauté the celery and eggplant for 5 minutes. Add the zucchini and sauté for another 2–3 minutes.

ADD THE VEGETABLES, rice, and remaining stock to the cooker, lock the lid in place, and bring up to low pressure, 8psi, and cook for 5–10 more minutes. Use the quick release method, carefully remove the lid, and season with salt and pepper.

SERVE IN A BOWL and sprinkle with parsley.

SERVES 4

Chicken Soup

3 lb boneless chicken breasts
    and thighs
1 medium onion, quartered
2 celery stalks, sliced
3 carrots, sliced
2 sprigs parsley
3 sprigs thyme
1 bay leaf
6 black peppercorns
4 cups chicken stock
Parsley for garnish
Kosher salt

RINSE THE CHICKEN and pat dry. Place all of the ingredients in a pressure cooker and season with salt.

LOCK THE COOKER'S LID in place, and bring up to high pressure, 15psi, according to manufacturer's directions. When pressure is reached, lower the heat and cook for 10 minutes. Adjust the heat as necessary to maintain even cooking pressure. Allow the pressure to drop using the cold water or quick release method and carefully remove the lid.

SERVE CHICKEN SOUP in warm bowls and garnish with chopped parsley.

SERVES 4

Chicken Curry

4 lb assorted chicken pieces

3 tbs peanut oil or ghee

1 cup white onions, chopped

2 garlic cloves

1½ tsp freshly grated ginger

2 tbs curry powder

1 tsp chili powder

15 oz diced tomatoes

2 tbs chopped cilantro

1 cup chicken stock

1 tsp garam masala

½ cup plain yogurt

3 tbs sliced green onions

Cilantro for sprinkling

Kosher salt

RINSE THE CHICKEN and pat dry. Heat the oil or ghee in a pressure cooker and brown the chicken on all sides; remove, and set aside. Add the onions, garlic, and ginger and sauté 3–5 minutes. Add the curry and chili powder and stir together. Add the tomatoes, cilantro, and stock; return the chicken and season with salt.

COVER THE PRESSURE COOKER with the lid, lock it in place, and bring up to high pressure, 15psi, according to manufacturer's directions. When high pressure is reached, lower the heat and cook for 10 minutes. Adjust the heat as necessary to maintain even cooking pressure. Allow the pressure to drop using the quick release or cold water method and carefully remove the lid.

STIR IN THE GARAM MASALA, yogurt, and green onions and simmer gently for 5 minutes.

SERVE OVER RICE with additional cilantro sprinkled on the top.

SERVES 6

TIP

▶ Garam masala is an Indian spice blend found in most Asian or Indian grocery stores.

Chicken and Bell Peppers

3½ lb assorted chicken pieces
1 tbs ghee (or clarified butter)
½ cup onions, chopped
2 garlic cloves, minced
2 tbs tomato paste
2 tbs Hungarian sweet paprika
1 cup chicken stock
1 cup red and green bell
    peppers, diced
½ cup sour cream
1 tbs chopped parsley
Kosher salt
Freshly ground black pepper

RINSE THE CHICKEN, pat dry, and season with salt and pepper. Heat the ghee or clarified butter in a pressure cooker and brown the chicken on all sides; remove, and set aside. Add the onions and garlic, and sauté 3–5 minutes. Stir in the tomato paste, paprika, stock, bell peppers, and reserved chicken.

COVER THE PRESSURE COOKER, lock the lid into place, and bring up to high pressure, 15psi, according to manufacturer's directions. When pressure is reached, lower the heat and cook for 10 minutes. Adjust the heat as necessary to maintain even cooking pressure. Allow the pressure to drop using the quick release or cold water method and carefully remove the lid.

USING A SLOTTED SPOON, remove the chicken and arrange it on a platter.

IN A BOWL, stir the sour cream into a little bit of the sauce until smooth, then carefully add to the rest of the sauce in the cooker, stirring constantly. Simmer to reduce slightly and season to taste with salt and pepper.

TO SERVE: Drizzle half of the sauce over the top of the chicken or serve the rest on the side. Garnish with parsley.

SERVES 6

Lemon Thyme Chicken

2½ lb assorted chicken pieces
3 tbs sunflower oil
½ cup pearl onions, peeled
   and chopped
½ cup red bell peppers, diced
3 garlic cloves, minced
½ cup dry white wine
½ cup chicken stock
1 tbs chopped lemon thyme
Zest from 1 lemon
Juice from ½ lemon
½ lemon, sliced into 4 pieces
Kosher salt
Freshly ground black pepper

RINSE THE CHICKEN, pat dry, and season with salt and pepper. Heat the oil in a pressure cooker and brown the chicken on all sides; remove, and set aside. Add the onions, bell peppers, and garlic and sauté 3–5 minutes. Add the wine and stock and bring to a boil. Stir in the thyme, lemon zest, and lemon juice. Return the reserved chicken and season with salt and pepper.

COVER THE PRESSURE COOKER, lock the lid into place, and bring up to high pressure, 15psi, according to manufacturer's directions. When pressure is reached, lower the heat and cook for 8–10 minutes. Allow the pressure to drop using the quick release or cold water method and carefully remove the lid.

TO SERVE: Arrange the chicken on a platter. Drizzle some of the juices over the top and garnish with lemon slices.

SERVES 4

Chicken Chili con Carne

2 lb skinless, boneless
   chicken thighs
½ cup vegetable oil
3 tbs diced medium-hot red
   chili peppers, seeds removed
½ cup onions, chopped
1 garlic clove, minced
½ cup red bell peppers, seeds
   removed and diced
8 oz diced tomatoes
16 oz can red kidney beans
3 tsp Hungarian sweet paprika
1 tbs tomato paste
1½ cups chicken stock
1 tsp chopped thyme
1 tsp chopped oregano
Kosher salt
Freshly ground white pepper

RINSE THE CHICKEN, pat dry, cut into ½ inch cubes, and season with salt and pepper.

HEAT THE OIL in a pressure cooker and brown the chicken on all sides; remove, and set aside. Add the chili peppers, onions, garlic, and bell pepper and sauté 3–5 minutes. Add the tomatoes, kidney beans, paprika, tomato paste, stock, thyme, oregano, return the chicken, and season with salt and pepper.

COVER THE PRESSURE COOKER, lock the lid into place, and bring up to high pressure, 15psi, according to manufacturer's directions. When pressure is reached, lower the heat and cook for 5–7 minutes. Adjust the heat as necessary to maintain even cooking pressure. Allow the pressure to drop using the quick release or cold water method and carefully remove the lid.

SERVE CHILI in bowls with tortilla chips on the side.

SERVES 4

Turkey with Gravy

2 lb turkey drumsticks
   and thighs
½ cup celery, chopped
½ cup carrots, chopped
½ cup onions, chopped
3 sprigs parsley
6 peppercorns
1 bay leaf
4 cups chicken stock
Parsley for garnish
Kosher salt
Freshly ground black pepper

RINSE THE TURKEY, pat dry, and season with salt and pepper. Place the turkey and the rest of the ingredients in the pressure cooker.

COVER, LOCK THE LID IN PLACE, and bring up to high pressure, 15psi, according to manufacturer's directions. Once pressure is reached, lower the heat and cook for 10–15 minutes. Adjust the heat as necessary to maintain even cooking pressure. Allow the pressure to drop naturally and carefully remove the lid.

USING A SLOTTED SPOON, remove the turkey and vegetables and arrange on a platter. Pour the stock through a strainer into a sauce pan. Bring to a boil and reduce slightly, season to taste with salt and pepper.

TO SERVE: Drizzle some of the gravy over the turkey and vegetables and serve the rest on the side. Garnish with chopped parsley.

SERVES 2

Duck Soup with Cannellini Beans

1 cup dried cannellini beans
½ lb duck breast and thighs
2 tbs olive oil
½ cup onions, chopped
3 oz bacon
1 tsp chopped marjoram
4 cups chicken stock
Marjoram for garnish
Kosher salt
Freshly ground black pepper

PLACE THE CANNELLINI BEANS in a bowl, cover with cold water, and soak overnight.

THE NEXT DAY, pour the beans into a strainer, draining the water, and rinse thoroughly.

PLACE THE BEANS in a pressure cooker with 4 cups of salted water, cover, lock the lid into place and bring up to high pressure, 15psi, according to manufacturer's directions. When pressure is reached, lower the heat and cook for 6–8 minutes. Allow the pressure to drop naturally, carefully remove the lid, and remove the beans. Set the beans aside in a bowl and rinse the cooker.

RINSE THE DUCK and pat dry. Using a sharp knife, cut the duck into 1 inch cubes, and season with salt and pepper. Heat the oil in the pressure cooker and brown the duck on all sides. Add the onions and bacon and sauté 3–5 minutes, then add the marjoram and stock.

COVER THE PRESSURE COOKER with the lid, lock it in place, and bring up to high pressure, 15psi, according to manufacturer's directions. When pressure is reached, lower the heat and cook for 10–15 minutes. Adjust the heat as necessary to maintain even cooking pressure. Allow the pressure to drop naturally and carefully remove the lid. Stir in the reserved cannellini beans.

SERVE THE SOUP in warm bowls garnished with marjoram and crusty bread on the side.

SERVES 2

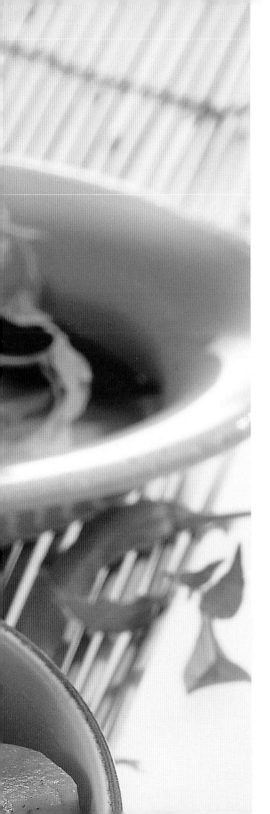

RICE AND VEGETABLES

NO DIET IS COMPLETE without rice, grains, and vegetables. And the closer the food is to its raw, or natural state, the more nutritious. In a time when so much of what we consume is processed or refined, the pressure cooker retains the nutrients and vitamins without sacrificing flavor.

Making perfect rice and grains every time is an obtainable goal when pressure cooking. All it takes are 4 simple steps.... 1. Add rice and cooking liquid to the cooker. 2. Bring the liquid to a boil and lock the lid into place. 3. Let the pressure drop naturally, and 4. Fluff and serve!

Pressure cooking vegetables keeps them fresh, colorful, and nutritious. If multiple vegetables are being cooked at the same time, cut them into similar sized pieces so cooking times will be the same. Keep vegetables crunchy by placing them on top of a trivet with cooking liquid underneath.

PRESSURE COOKER

Butternut Squash Risotto

2 tbs butter, separated
1 tbs olive oil
½ cup white onions, chopped
1 cup butternut squash, peeled
    and cubed
1 cup Arborio rice
⅔ cup dry white wine
3–5 saffron threads
2 cups vegetable stock, separated
½ cup baby spinach
½ cup freshly grated
    Parmigiano-Reggiano
Kosher salt
Freshly ground black pepper

HEAT 1 TABLESPOON of butter and olive oil in the pressure cooker. Add the onions and sauté for 2–3 minutes, being careful not to brown. Stir in the butternut squash and sauté 2–3 more minutes. Add the rice, stirring, and cook for 1 minute. Add the wine and saffron, stirring, until most of the wine is absorbed, and then add 1½ cups of stock and season with salt and pepper.

COVER THE PRESSURE COOKER, lock the lid into place, and bring up to high pressure, 15psi, according to manufacturer's directions. When pressure is reached, lower the heat and cook for 5–7 minutes. Adjust the heat as necessary to maintain even cooking pressure. Allow the pressure to drop naturally and carefully remove the lid.

ADD THE REMAINING STOCK, the remaining butter, stir in the spinach, and Parmigiano-Reggiano and season with salt and pepper.

FLUFF THE RISOTTO and serve immediately in warm bowls. Shave additional Parmigiano-Reggiano over the top.

SERVES 4

Zucchini Risotto

3 tbs olive oil
½ cup onions, chopped
⅓ cup zucchini, sliced
1 cup Arborio rice
⅔ cup dry white wine
2 cups vegetable stock, separated
2 tbs unsalted butter
1 tsp chopped thyme leaves
½ cup freshly grated
    Parmigiano-Reggiano
Thyme for garnish
Kosher salt
Freshly ground white pepper

HEAT THE OLIVE OIL in the pressure cooker. Add the onions and sauté for 2–3 minutes, being careful not to brown. Stir in the zucchini and sauté 2–3 more minutes. Add the rice, stirring, and cook for 1 minute. Add the wine and stir until most of it is absorbed, then add 1½ cups of stock, and season with salt and pepper.

COVER THE PRESSURE COOKER, lock the lid in place, and bring up to high pressure, 15psi, according to manufacturer's directions. When pressure is reached, lower the heat and cook for 5–7 minutes. Adjust the heat as necessary to maintain even cooking pressure. Allow the pressure to drop naturally and carefully remove the lid.

ADD THE REMAINING STOCK and butter. Stir in the thyme and Parmigiano-Reggiano, and season with salt and pepper.

FLUFF THE RISOTTO and serve immediately in warm bowls, garnishing with additional thyme, and crusty Italian bread on the side.

SERVES 4

Cherry Pilaf

1 tbs butter
2 tbs chopped white onions
½ cup long-grain rice
1 cup vegetable stock
½ tsp fennel seeds
½ cup sour dried cherries
Basil leaves for garnish
Kosher salt
Freshly ground white pepper

MELT THE BUTTER in a pressure cooker and sauté the onions for 2–4 minutes. Add the rice and sauté for 1 more minute. Add the stock and fennel seeds and season with salt and pepper.

COVER THE PRESSURE COOKER, lock the lid into place, and bring up to high pressure, 15psi, according to manufacturer's directions. When pressure is reached, lower the heat and cook for 5 minutes. Adjust the heat as necessary to maintain even cooking pressure. Allow the pressure to drop naturally and carefully remove the lid.

STIR IN THE CHERRIES and season with salt and pepper.

TO SERVE: Fluff the rice and garnish with basil leaves.

SERVES 4

Brown Rice Bowl

2 tbs olive oil
½ cup carrots, sliced
1 leek, white parts only, cut
    into strips
1 bell pepper, cut into strips
½ cup white cabbage, cut
    into strips
1 cup long-grain brown rice
1½ cups vegetable stock
½ cup bean sprouts
1 tbs soy sauce
2 tsp curry powder
Kosher salt
Freshly ground black pepper

HEAT THE OIL in the bottom of the pressure cooker and sauté the carrots, leek, bell pepper, and cabbage for 5–7 minutes. Season with salt and pepper, then add the rice, and stock.

COVER THE PRESSURE COOKER, lock the lid in place, and bring up to low pressure, 8psi, according to manufacturer's directions. When pressure is reached, lower the heat and cook for 20 minutes. Adjust the heat as necessary to maintain even cooking pressure. Allow the pressure to drop naturally and carefully remove the lid.

STIR IN THE BEAN SPROUTS, soy sauce, and curry. Fluff the rice, scoop into bowls, and serve immediately.

SERVES 4

Jamaican Coat
of Arms

1 cup gungo peas (pigeon peas)
3 cups unsweetened coconut milk
2 tbs chopped shallots
1 cup long-grain rice
1 cup vegetable stock
1 tbs chopped thyme
Kosher salt
Freshly ground white pepper

RINSE THE PEAS well and drain. Place the peas and coconut milk in a pressure cooker. Cover, lock the cooker's lid in place, and bring up to high pressure, 15psi, according to manufacturer's directions. When pressure is reached, lower the heat and cook for 8–10 minutes. Adjust the heat as necessary to maintain even cooking pressure. Allow the pressure to drop naturally and carefully remove the lid.

ADD THE SHALLOTS, rice, stock, and thyme and stir all of the ingredients until combined. Cover the pressure cooker again, lock the lid in place, bring to low pressure, 8psi, and cook for 8–10 more minutes, adjusting the heat to maintain even pressure. Allow the pressure to drop naturally and remove the lid.

FLUFF THE RICE and peas and serve immediately in warm bowls or as a side dish.

SERVES 4

Boston Baked Beans

1 cup large dried white beans
½ lb salt pork or bacon, diced
½ cup onions, chopped
3 garlic cloves, minced
1 tsp dry, yellow mustard
½ tsp cinnamon
½ tsp cloves
1 tbs molasses
1 tbs red wine vinegar
2 tbs tomato paste
15 oz diced tomatoes
1 cup chicken stock
1 tbs chopped parsley
Kosher salt
Freshly ground black pepper

COVER THE BEANS with cold water and soak overnight. The next day, drain and rinse.

HEAT THE PRESSURE COOKER and sauté the salt pork or bacon until crispy. Add the onions and garlic and sauté for 3–5 minutes. Stir in the mustard, cinnamon, cloves, molasses, vinegar, tomato paste, tomatoes, stock, and beans and season with salt and pepper.

COVER THE PRESSURE COOKER, lock the lid into place, and bring up to low pressure, 8psi, according to manufacturer's directions. When pressure is reached, lower the heat and cook for 20 minutes. Adjust the heat as necessary to maintain even cooking pressure. Allow the pressure to drop naturally or use the quick release method and carefully remove the lid.

BEFORE SERVING, stir the beans, season with salt and pepper, and garnish with parsley.

SERVES 2

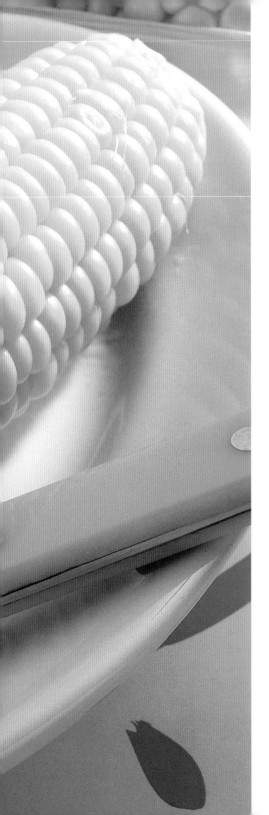

Corn on the Cob

4 fresh ears of corn, shucked
3–4 tbs unsalted butter
½ tsp kosher salt
½ cup water

PLACE THE TRIVET in the bottom of the pressure cooker and add the corn, butter, salt, and water.

COVER AND LOCK the cooker's lid into place. Bring up to high pressure, 15psi, according to manufacturer's directions. When pressure is reached, lower the heat and cook for 3 minutes. Allow the pressure to drop, using the cold water release method and carefully remove the lid.

SERVES 4

Cauliflower Curry

½ cup vegetable oil

1 tbs panch phoran

½ cup green onions, sliced
    into rings

1 lb red new potatoes, peeled
    and halved

1 cauliflower, cut into florets

2 chili peppers, seeds removed
    and cut into strips

2 tsp turmeric

1 tsp cumin

2 tsp Hungarian sweet paprika

1 tbs grated ginger root

1½ cups vegetable stock

8 oz diced tomatoes

⅔ cup peas

¼ cup yogurt

1 tsp garam masala

1 tbs chopped cilantro

Kosher salt

Freshly ground black pepper

IN A PRESSURE COOKER, heat the oil and braise panch phoran while stirring until it becomes aromatic. Add the onions and sauté 2–3 minutes. Add potatoes, cauliflower, and chili peppers and sauté over medium heat for 3–4 minutes. Stir in the turmeric, cumin, paprika, and ginger. Season with salt and pepper and sauté for 3–4 more minutes.

ADD THE STOCK. Lock the cooker's lid into place and bring up to high pressure, 15psi, according to manufacturer's directions. When pressure is reached, lower the heat and cook for 2–3 minutes. Adjust the heat as necessary to maintain even cooking pressure. Allow the pressure to drop using the cold water release method and carefully remove the lid.

STIR IN THE TOMATOES and peas and simmer for 3–5 minutes, then remove from the heat, and stir in the yogurt and garam masala.

SERVE IN A BOWL or as a side dish with cilantro sprinkled over the top.

SERVES 4

TIP

▶ Panch phoron is an Indian five-spice mixture and an important flavoring in this curry dish. It is comprised of mustard seeds, fennel seeds, cumin, onion seeds, and fenugreek seeds. You can find this spice blend in Asian grocery stores.

Ratatouille

2 tbs olive oil
½ cup onions, chopped
1 garlic clove, minced
⅔ cup eggplant, cubed
½ cup zucchini, cubed
⅓ cup red bell peppers, cubed
⅓ cup yellow bell peppers, cubed
½ cup beefsteak tomatoes, seeds
    removed and cubed
½ cup vegetable stock
1 tsp dried thyme
Several basil leaves
Kosher salt
Freshly ground black pepper

HEAT THE OLIVE OIL in a pressure cooker. Add the onions and garlic and sauté for 3–5 minutes. Add the vegetables and stock, stir in the thyme, and season with salt and pepper.

COVER THE COOKER and lock the lid into place. Bring up to high pressure, 15psi, according to manufacturer's directions. When pressure is reached, lower the heat and cook for 3–5 minutes. Adjust the heat as necessary to maintain even cooking pressure. Allow the pressure to drop using the cold water release method and carefully remove the lid.

SERVE RATATOUILLE in a bowl garnished with basil leaves.

Italian Brussels Sprouts

2 lb Brussels sprouts
2 tbs olive oil
2 oz bacon
2 tbs chopped onions
1 cup red and yellow tomatoes,
    seeds removed and diced
1 tbs chopped basil
2 tbs freshly grated
    Parmigiano-Reggiano
Kosher salt
Freshly ground black pepper

CLEAN THE BRUSSELS SPROUTS by removing the outer leaves, trimming the cores, and scoring them with an X. Place them on the trivet in a pressure cooker with ½ cup of water.

COVER AND LOCK THE LID into place. Bring up to high pressure, 15psi, according to manufacturer's directions. When pressure is reached, lower the heat and cook for 3–4 minutes. Adjust the heat as necessary to maintain even cooking pressure. Allow the pressure to drop using the cold release method and carefully remove the lid.

IN A PAN, heat the olive oil and brown the bacon and onions while stirring. Add Brussels sprouts and sauté for 3–4 minutes. Add tomatoes and basil and sauté for 2–3 more minutes. Season with salt and pepper and serve with Parmigiano-Reggiano.

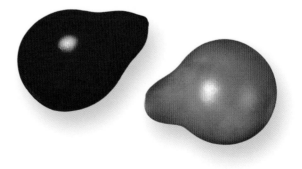

SOUPS AND STEWS

MAKING SOUPS AND STEWS in a pressure cooker is simple and takes minutes opposed to hours in a stockpot on the stovetop. Recipes in this chapter feature a flavored stock—the primary building block for a flavorful soup, aromatic vegetables such as onions, leeks, garlic, shallots, carrots and celery, and herbs and spices that add subtle nuances and complement key flavors. Whole spices like peppercorns, bay leaves and cinnamon sticks are removed after cooking, and chopped herbs like parsley, basil, and cilantro make for a perfect garnish. Always use salt to season and enhance flavor. And remember, fill the cooker no more than half full, especially when cooking with ingredients that will expand or foam like beans and split peas.

Carrot Ginger Soup

2 tbs vegetable oil
2 tbs green onions, cut into rings
1 red chili pepper, seeds removed
    and cut into rings
2 tsp freshly grated ginger root
1 tsp lemon grass, cut into rings
2 cups carrots, julienned
2 tbs chopped celery
4 cups vegetable stock
1 kaffir lime leaf (fresh or dried)
1 tbs chopped cilantro
Kosher salt
Freshly ground black pepper

HEAT THE OIL in a pressure cooker and sauté the onions, chili pepper, ginger, and lemon grass for 2–3 minutes. Add the carrots, celery, stock, and lime leaf, and season to taste with salt and pepper.

COVER THE PRESSURE COOKER and lock the lid into place. Bring up to high pressure, 15psi, according to manufacturer's directions. When pressure is reached, lower the heat and cook for 5 minutes. Adjust the heat as necessary to maintain even cooking pressure. Allow the pressure to drop naturally or use the quick release method and carefully remove the lid.

SEASON TO TASTE with salt and pepper and garnish with cilantro.

SERVES 4

Tomato Basil Soup

2 tbs extra-virgin olive oil
½ cup onions, chopped
1 garlic clove, minced
½ cup carrots, diced
2 tbs chopped celery
½ cup parsley, chopped
5 whole basil leaves
1 lb beefsteak tomatoes, seeds
    removed and chopped
3 cups vegetable stock
Basil for garnish
Kosher salt
Freshly ground white pepper

IN A PRESSURE COOKER, heat the oil and sauté the onions and garlic 2–3 minutes. Add the carrots, celery, parsley, and basil and sauté for 2–3 more minutes, stirring. Add the tomatoes and stock, and season with salt and pepper.

COVER THE PRESSURE COOKER and lock the lid into place. Bring up to high pressure, 15psi, according to manufacturers directions. When pressure is reached, lower the heat and cook for 5–7 minutes. Adjust the heat as necessary to maintain even cooking pressure. Allow the pressure to drop naturally or use the quick release method and carefully remove the lid.

REMOVE THE COOKER from the heat, purée the soup with a hand blender, and pour it through a chinois or fine strainer. Return it to the cooker to reheat and season with salt and pepper.

SERVE IN WARM BOWLS garnished with basil leaves.

SERVES 4

Cream of Broccoli Soup

1 lb broccoli, cut into florets
½ cup carrots, sliced
2½ cups vegetable stock
⅓ cup heavy cream
Pinch of grated nutmeg
Nutmeg for garnish
Kosher salt
Freshly ground black pepper

COMBINE THE BROCCOLI, carrots, and stock in a pressure cooker.

COVER AND LOCK the cooker's lid into place. Bring up to high pressure, 15psi, according to manufacturers directions. When pressure is reached, lower the heat and cook for 3–5 minutes. Adjust the heat as necessary to maintain even cooking pressure. Allow the pressure to drop naturally or use the quick release method and carefully remove the lid.

REMOVE THE COOKER from the heat and stir in the cream and nutmeg and season with salt and pepper.

SERVE THE SOUP in warm bowls with a dash of nutmeg.

SERVES 4

Pea Soup with Mint Croutons

Pea soup

2 tbs olive oil

½ cup onions, chopped

⅔ cup petite peas (frozen)

3 cups vegetable stock

½ cup heavy cream

Pinch of curry powder

Croutons

1 tbs butter

2 slices stale white bread,
    cubed into ½ inch pieces

1 tbs chopped mint leaves

Mint leaves for garnish

Kosher salt

Freshly ground white pepper

HEAT THE OLIVE OIL in a pressure cooker and sauté the onions for 2–3 minutes. Add the peas, stirring for 1 minute then add the stock.

COVER AND LOCK the cooker's lid into place. Bring up to low pressure, 8psi, according to manufacturer's directions. When pressure is reached, lower the heat and cook for 3–5 minutes. Adjust the heat as necessary to maintain even cooking pressure. Allow the pressure to drop naturally or use the quick release method and carefully remove the lid.

REMOVE THE COOKER from the heat and purée the soup with a hand blender. Stir in the cream and curry powder and season to taste with salt and pepper.

TO MAKE THE CROUTONS: Heat the butter in a pan and add the bread. Sprinkle with a little salt and add the mint leaves. Sauté until the bread is golden brown.

REHEAT THE PEA SOUP before serving and pour it into bowls. Garnish with croutons and mint leaves.

SERVES 4

Cauliflower Soup

2 tbs olive oil
2 tbs chopped onions
⅔ lb cauliflower florets
4 cups vegetable stock
Pinch of grated nutmeg
1 tsp lemon juice
1 egg yolk
1 tsp heavy cream
1 tbs chopped parsley
Kosher salt
Freshly ground white pepper

HEAT THE OLIVE OIL in a pressure cooker and sauté the onions for 2–3 minutes. Add the cauliflower and stock.

COVER AND LOCK the cooker's lid into place. Bring up to low pressure, 8psi, according to manufacturers directions. When pressure is reached, lower the heat and cook for 3–5 minutes. Adjust the heat as necessary to maintain even cooking pressure. Allow the pressure to drop naturally or use the quick release method and carefully remove the lid.

REMOVE THE COOKER from the heat. Using a slotted spoon, remove about ½ cup of cauliflower florets. Using a hand blender, purée the soup. Stir in the nutmeg, lemon juice, and cauliflower florets and season with salt and pepper.

IN A BOWL, combine the egg yolk and cream. Pour into the soup, stirring to thicken. Season to taste with salt and pepper and garnish with parsley.

SERVES 4

Swiss Chard Soup

2 tbs olive oil
½ cup onions, chopped
½ cup white turnips, peeled
    and diced
½ cup carrots, diced
½ cup red new potatoes, diced
½ cup ham, diced
5 cups vegetable stock
½ lb Swiss chard, cut into strips
8 oz diced tomatoes
1 tbs chopped parsley
Kosher salt
Freshly ground black pepper

HEAT THE OLIVE OIL in a pressure cooker and sauté the onions for 2–3 minutes. Add the turnips, carrots, potatoes, ham, and stock.

COVER AND LOCK the cooker's lid into place. Bring up to high pressure, 15psi, according to manufacturer's directions. When pressure is reached, lower the heat and cook for 3–5 minutes. Adjust the heat as necessary to maintain even cooking pressure. Allow the pressure to drop naturally or use the quick release method and carefully remove the lid.

STIR IN THE CHARD and tomatoes; simmer for 3–5 minutes until the chard wilts and season with salt and pepper.

SERVE SWISS CHARD SOUP in warm bowls sprinkled with parsley.

SERVES 6

Cream of Green Bean Soup

2 oz bacon, diced
3 tbs onions, chopped
⅔ lb green beans, ends trimmed
    and cut into 2 inch pieces
3 cups vegetable stock
1 tbs chopped parsley
⅔ cup heavy cream
1 tbs white balsamic vinegar
Parsley for garnish
Kosher salt
Freshly ground black pepper

HEAT THE PRESSURE COOKER and add the bacon. Cook until it starts to get crispy, 3–5 minutes then add the onions and sauté for 2–3 more minutes. Add the green beans and the stock and season with salt and pepper.

COVER AND LOCK the cooker's lid into place. Bring up to low pressure, 8psi, according to manufacturer's directions. When pressure is reached, lower the heat and cook for 2–3 minutes. Adjust the heat as necessary to maintain even cooking pressure. Allow the pressure to drop naturally or use the quick release method and carefully remove the lid.

STIR IN THE PARSLEY, cream, and vinegar. Simmer for 5 minutes and season with salt and pepper.

SERVE CREAM OF GREEN BEAN SOUP in warm bowls garnished with parsley.

SERVES 4

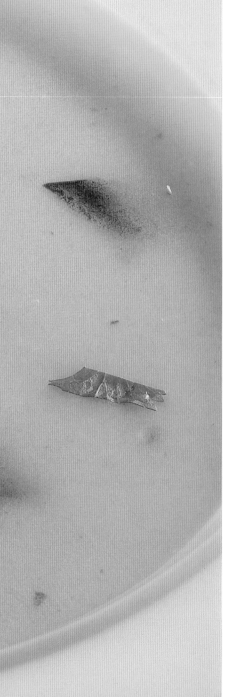

Spicy Squash Soup

2 tbs peanut oil
½ cup white onions, chopped
2 garlic cloves, minced
½ cup carrots, chopped
2 tsp ginger root, grated
1½ lb butternut or kabocha
    squash, peeled and diced
1 tsp red pepper flakes
1 tsp mild madras curry powder
4 cups vegetable stock
½ cup heavy cream
½ cup red bell peppers, diced
1 tbs chopped cilantro
Cilantro for garnish
Kosher salt
Freshly ground black pepper

HEAT THE OIL in the pressure cooker. Add the onions and garlic and sauté for 2–3 minutes, then add the carrots, ginger, and squash. Add the red pepper flakes, curry, and stock and season with salt and pepper.

COVER AND LOCK the cooker's lid into place. Bring up to high pressure, 15psi, according to manufacturer's directions. When pressure is reached, lower the heat and cook for 5–7 minutes. Adjust the heat as necessary to maintain even cooking pressure. Allow the pressure to drop naturally or use the quick release method and carefully remove the lid.

REMOVE THE COOKER from the heat and purée with a hand blender. Stir in the cream, bell peppers, and cilantro and season to taste with salt and pepper.

SERVE SPICY SQUASH SOUP in bowls and garnish with additional cilantro.

SERVES 4

Moroccan Lentil Stew

3 tbs olive oil
½ cup onions, chopped
2 fresh chili peppers, seeds
    removed and diced
1 tbs Hungarian sweet paprika
½ tsp cayenne pepper
1 tsp cumin
1 cup dried lentils
15 oz diced tomatoes
2 lb kabocha squash, cubed
1½ cups vegetable stock
2 cups red or green Swiss chard,
    ribs removed and shredded
1 tbs chopped cilantro
Kosher salt
Freshly ground black pepper

IN A PRESSURE COOKER, heat the oil and sauté the onions and chili peppers for 3–5 minutes. Stir in the paprika, cayenne pepper, cumin, lentils, tomatoes, squash, and stock and season with salt.

COVER THE PRESSURE COOKER and lock the lid into place. Bring up to high pressure, 15psi, according to manufacturer's directions. When pressure is reached, lower the heat and cook for 7–10 minutes. Adjust the heat as necessary to maintain even cooking pressure. Allow the pressure to drop naturally and carefully remove the lid.

STIR IN THE CHARD until wilted and season to taste with salt and pepper.

SERVE MOROCCAN LENTIL STEW in warm bowls garnished with cilantro.

SERVES 4

Bean Stew with Herb-Parmesan Croutons

Bean Stew

⅓ cup dried white beans
⅓ cup dried brown beans
4 oz bacon or salt pork, diced
½ cup white onions, chopped
2 garlic cloves, minced
½ cup celery, chopped
½ cup carrots, sliced
½ cup leeks, white parts only,
    sliced into rings
2 cups green beans, ends and
    strings removed
8 oz diced tomatoes
1 bay leaf
3 cloves
Pinch of allspice

Croutons

2 slices stale white bread
3 tbs olive oil
1 tbs grated Parmigiano-Reggiano
1 tsp chopped parsley
Parsley for garnish
Parmigiano-Reggiano for garnish
Kosher salt
Freshly ground black pepper

COVER THE BEANS so they are thoroughly submerged in water over night. The next day, rinse them and drain.

HEAT THE PRESSURE COOKER on the stovetop and add the bacon or salt pork. Cook it until crispy, then remove, and sauté the onions and garlic in the grease. Stir in the celery, carrots, and leeks and add the beans with 1–1½ cup of their soaking water.

COVER AND LOCK the cooker's lid into place. Bring up to high pressure, 15psi, according to manufacturer's directions. When pressure is reached, lower the heat and cook for 10–12 minutes. Adjust the heat as necessary to maintain even cooking pressure. Allow the pressure to drop naturally and carefully remove the lid.

STIR IN THE GREEN BEANS, tomatoes, bay leaf, cloves, and allspice. Cover once again and bring up to high pressure 3–5 more minutes. Allow the pressure to drop naturally and carefully remove the lid.

TO MAKE THE CROUTONS: Remove the crust from the bread and cut into uniform ½ inch cubes. Heat the olive oil in a pan and toast the bread until golden brown. Sprinkle with Parmigiano-Reggiano and parsley, stirring so nothing burns.

SERVE THE STEW in soup bowls with croutons on the top. Garnish with additional chopped parsley and grated Parmigiano-Reggiano.

SERVES 4

Ceci Bean Stew

1 cup dried garbanzo beans
2 tbs olive oil
½ cup onions, chopped
3 garlic cloves, minced
2 tbs celery, chopped
1 tsp cumin
1 tsp fenugreek seeds
1 tsp brown sugar
½ tsp turmeric
Juice from ½ lemon
1 cup vegetable stock
1 tsp red pepper flakes
8 oz diced tomatoes
½ cup baby spinach
2 tbs chopped parsley
Kosher salt
Freshly ground white pepper

PLACE GARBANZO BEANS in a bowl, cover with cold water, and soak overnight.

THE NEXT DAY, rinse and drain the beans and transfer them to the pressure cooker with 2 cups of water.

LOCK THE COOKER'S LID into place and bring up to high pressure, 15psi, according to manufacturers directions. When pressure is reached, lower the heat and cook for 10–12 minutes. Adjust the heat as necessary to maintain even cooking pressure. Allow the pressure to drop naturally and carefully remove the lid. Put the beans in a bowl and set aside. Rinse the pressure cooker.

HEAT THE OLIVE OIL in the pressure cooker and add the onions and garlic. Sauté for 3–5 minutes, then add the celery, cumin, and fenugreek. Stir in the reserved garbanzo beans, brown sugar, turmeric, lemon juice, stock, red pepper flakes, and tomatoes. Cover once again and bring up to high pressure for 5–7 more minutes. Allow the pressure to drop naturally and remove the lid carefully.

STIR IN THE SPINACH until wilted and season with salt and pepper.

SERVE IN BOWLS garnished with parsley.

SERVES 4

INDEX